Date: 9/27/16

J 599.885 RIG
Riggs, Kate,
Chimpanzees /

Published by Creative Education
and Creative Paperbacks
P.O. Box 227, Mankato, Minnesota 56002
Creative Education and Creative Paperbacks
are imprints of The Creative Company
www.thecreativecompany.us

Design by The Design Lab
Production by Travis Green
Art direction by Rita Marshall
Printed in the United States of America

Photographs by Alamy (Juniors Bildarchiv GmbH),
Corbis (Gallo Images, Cyril Ruoso/JH Editorial/
Minden Pictures, Jürgen & Christine Sohns/
imageBROKER, Konrad Wothe/Minden Pictures),
Dreamstime (Sam D\'cruz, Kjersti Jorgensen, Smellme),
Science Source (Tom McHugh), Shutterstock (Nick
Biemans, Sergey Uryadnikov), SuperStock (Minden
Pictures, Steve Bloom Images/Steve Bloom Images)

Library of Congress Cataloging-in-Publication Data
Riggs, Kate.
Chimpanzees / Kate Riggs.
p. cm. — (Amazing animals)
Summary: A basic exploration of the appearance,
behavior, and habitat of chimpanzees, Africa's
intelligent primates. Also included is a story from
folklore explaining why chimpanzees do not have tails.
Includes bibliographical references and index.
ISBN 978-1-60818-610-5 (hardcover)
ISBN 978-1-62832-216-3 (pbk)
ISBN 978-1-56660-657-8 (eBook)
1. Chimpanzees—Juvenile literature. I. Title. II. Series:
Amazing animals.
QL737.P94R54 2016
599.885—dc23   2014048704

CCSS: RI.1.1, 2, 4, 5, 6, 7; RI.2.2, 5, 6, 7, 10;
RI.3.1, 5, 7, 8; RF.1.1, 3, 4; RF.2.3, 4

HC 9 8 7 6 5 4 3 2
First Edition PBK 9 8 7 6 5 4 3 2 1

AMAZING ANIMALS

CHIMPANZEES

BY KATE RIGGS

CREATIVE EDUCATION • CREATIVE PAPERBACKS

Chimpanzees live in 22 countries in Africa

Chimpanzees are **mammals** called primates. Monkeys, apes, and humans are primates, too. Four kinds of chimpanzees live in Africa. They live in grasslands and forests. They are named for where they live.

mammals animals that have hair or fur and feed their babies with milk

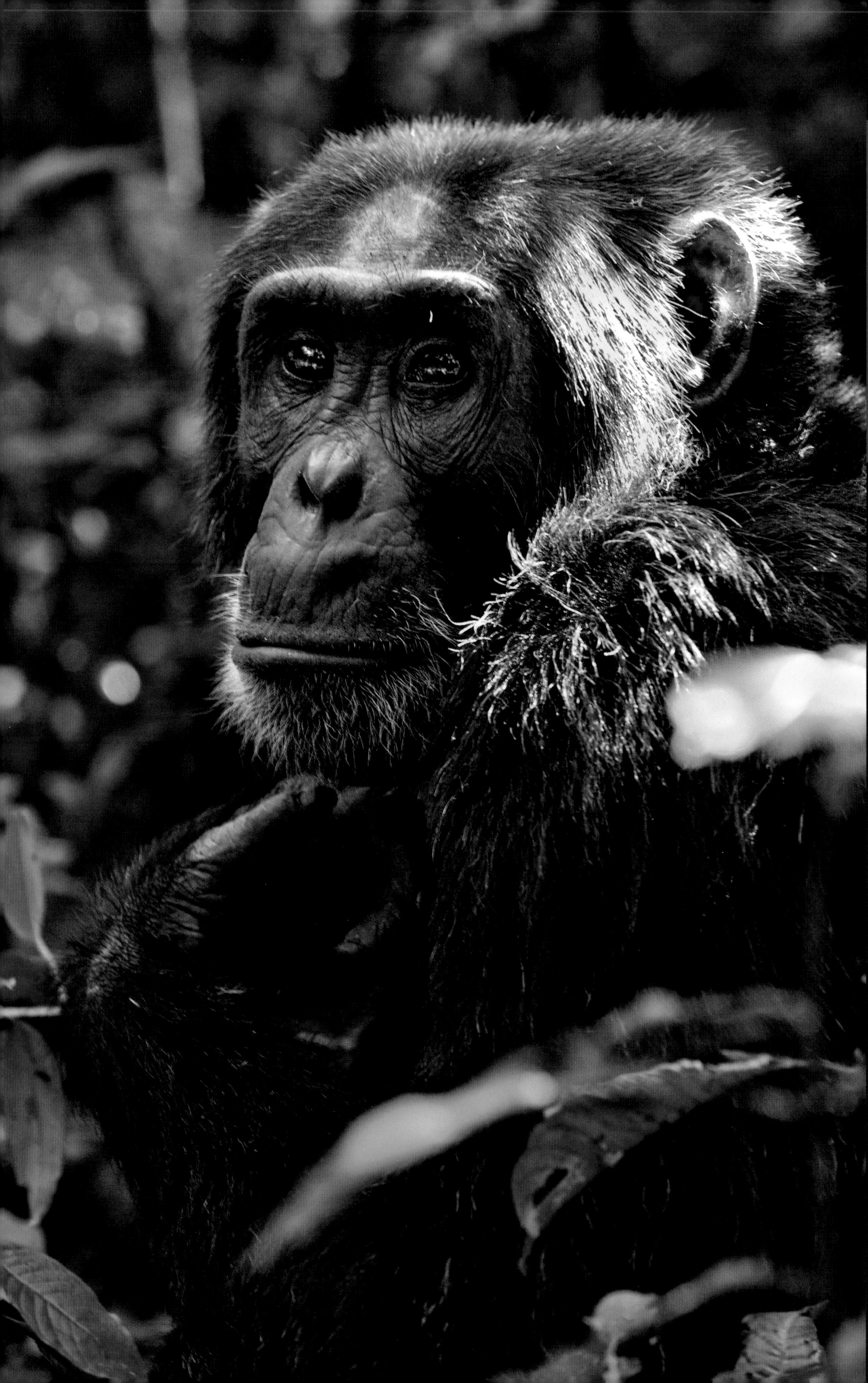

Chimps are smart primates.
They have big brains. Like other primates, they have thumbs that can grip. Their bodies are covered with black hair. The hair turns gray as the chimp ages.

Chimps do not have hair on their faces, hands, or feet

A male chimp is about four feet (1.2 m) tall. A female is shorter. Chimps have long arms. They like to walk on their knuckles. They use their long arms to swing through the trees.

Chimps walk on all fours with their knuckles and feet

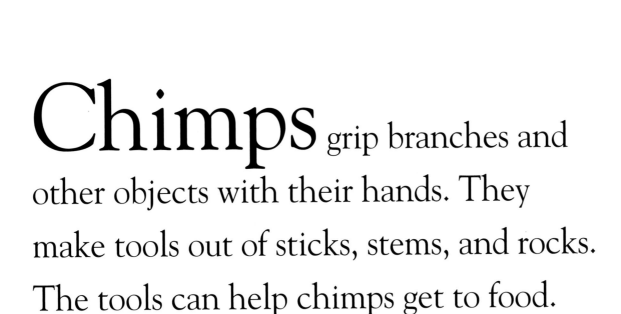

Chimps grip branches and other objects with their hands. They make tools out of sticks, stems, and rocks. The tools can help chimps get to food.

Chimps often use plant parts to gather and eat insects

Most chimps search for food alone or in small groups

A chimp will "fish" for termites. These insects live in mounds of dirt. Chimps that live in **rainforests** like to eat a lot of fruit. Chimps eat seeds, bark, and some animals, too.

rainforests forests with many trees and lots of rain

One baby chimpanzee is born at a time. A baby drinks milk from its mother. The mother teaches her young how to find food. Young chimps love to play. They learn how to get along with others. Chimps can live about 45 years in the wild.

Young chimps stay with their mother until age seven

Chimps call, kiss, hug, and make faces at one another

Fifteen to 150 chimps

live together in a group. Chimps in a **community** hoot at each other. They keep each other safe from **predators**. One male leads the community.

community a family group of chimpanzees

predators animals that kill and eat other animals

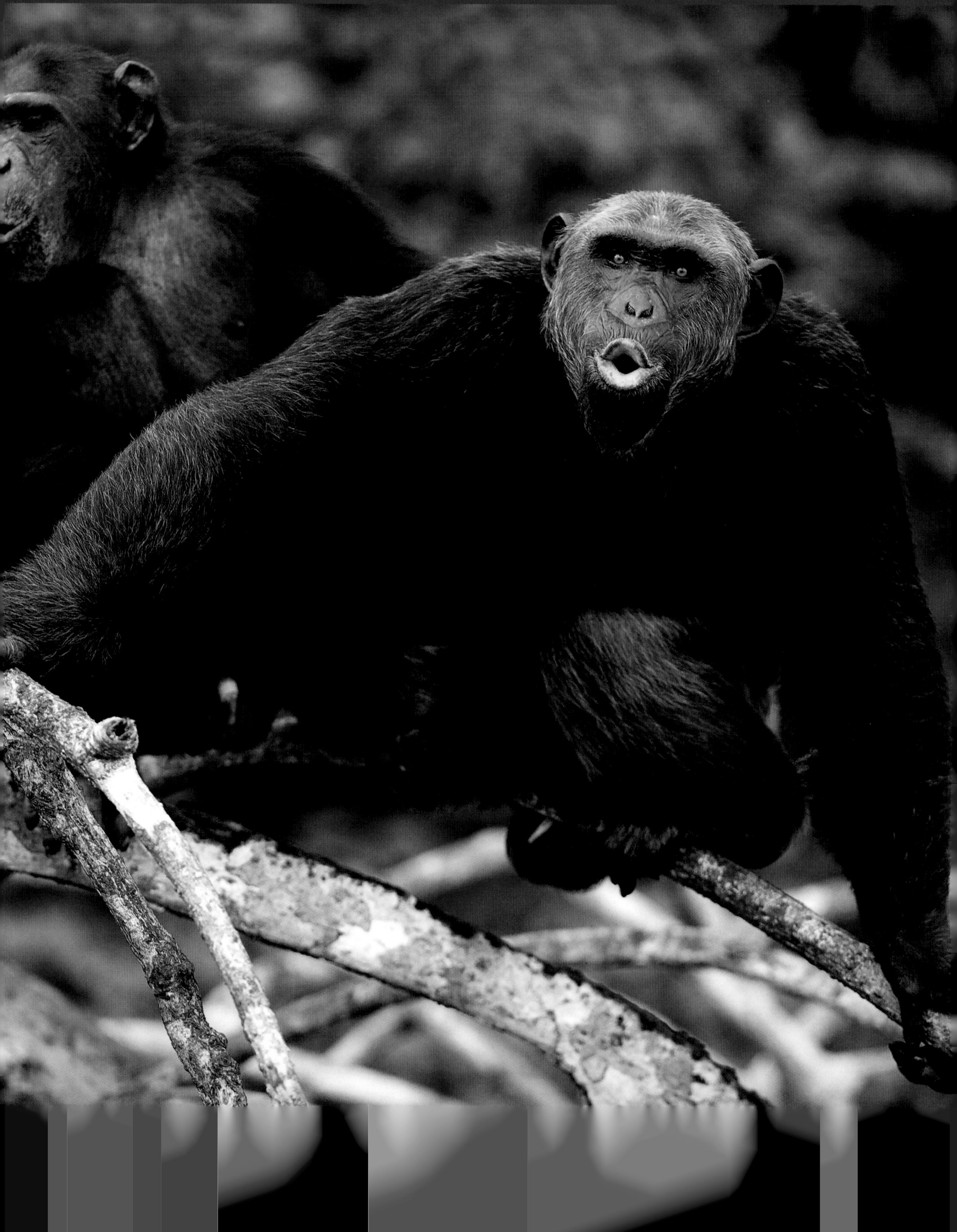

Chimps like to groom each other. They clean bugs and dirt out of their hair. Chimps make a lot of sounds to talk to one another. Every night, they build a new nest in the trees.

Grooming is an important part of life for all chimps

Chimpanzees are endangered animals. That means there are not many left in the wild. People can see chimps in zoos today. They like to watch these smart animals at work!

Many people today are working to keep chimps safe

A Chimpanzee Story

Why don't chimpanzees have tails? People in Africa told a story about this. Once, the chimpanzee had a long tail. Its tail helped it climb higher and reach the best food. The chimpanzee ate so much that other animals went hungry. An eagle took the tail one day, and the chimp has been without it ever since!

Read More

Depken, Kristen L. *Oscar and Freddy*. New York: Disney Press, 2012.

Kratt, Chris, and Martin Kratt. *To Be a Chimpanzee*. New York: Scholastic, 1997.

Websites

Animal Planet: Jane Goodall Playlist
*http://www.animalplanet.com/video-topics/wild-animals
/apes-and-other-primates-videos/jane-goodall.htm*
Watch videos about scientist Jane Goodall and her work with chimps.

Disneynature: Chimpanzee
http://nature.disney.com/chimpanzee
Learn more about the chimp named Oscar from the movie *Chimpanzee*.

Note: Every effort has been made to ensure that the websites listed above are suitable for children, that they have educational value, and that they contain no inappropriate material. However, because of the nature of the Internet, it is impossible to guarantee that these sites will remain active indefinitely or that their contents will not be altered.

Index